NAME

____

____

WHO DO YOU WANT TO BE
WHEN YOU GROW UP?

YOU CAN BE GOOD WITH NUMBERS
AND WORK IN A BANK

OR YOU COULD BE A BRAVE SOLDIER
AND FIGHT WITH A TANK

YOU CAN BE AN ASTRONAUT
AND FLY TO THE MOON

OR YOU CAN BE A MUSICIAN
AND MAKE YOUR OWN TUNE

YOU CAN BE A SPORTSMAN
AND SPEND YOUR TIME IN A FIELD

OR YOU CAN BE A LAWYER
AND MAKE THE TRUTH YOUR SHIELD

YOU CAN BE A SCIENTIST AND RESEARCH IN A LAB

OR YOU CAN BE AN ENGINEER
AND MAKE APPS FOR A TAB

YOU CAN BE A PILOT AND AIM TO FLY

OR YOU CAN BE A DOCTOR,TEACHER,
DANCER OR AN ENTREPRENEUR,

WHEREVER YOUR PASSION LIE.

NO MATTER WHAT YOU CHOOSE TO BE
MAKE SURE YOU LOVE WHAT YOU DO

BECAUSE YOU WILL BE THE BEST AT DOING WHATEVER YOUR HEART IS INTO

"You can be what you want to be"

Who do you want to be when you grow up?

You can be good with numbers and work in a bank
Or you could be a brave soldier and fight in/with a tank

You can be an astronaut and fly to the moon
Or you can be a musician and make your own tune

You can be a sportsman and spend your time in a field
Or you can be a lawyer and make the truth your shield

You can be a scientist and research in a lab
Or you can be an engineer and make apps for a tab

You can be a pilot and aim to fly
Or you can be a doctor, teacher, dancer or an entrepreneur,
wherever your passion lie

No matter what you choose to be, make sure you love what you do
Because you will be best at doing whatever your heart is into

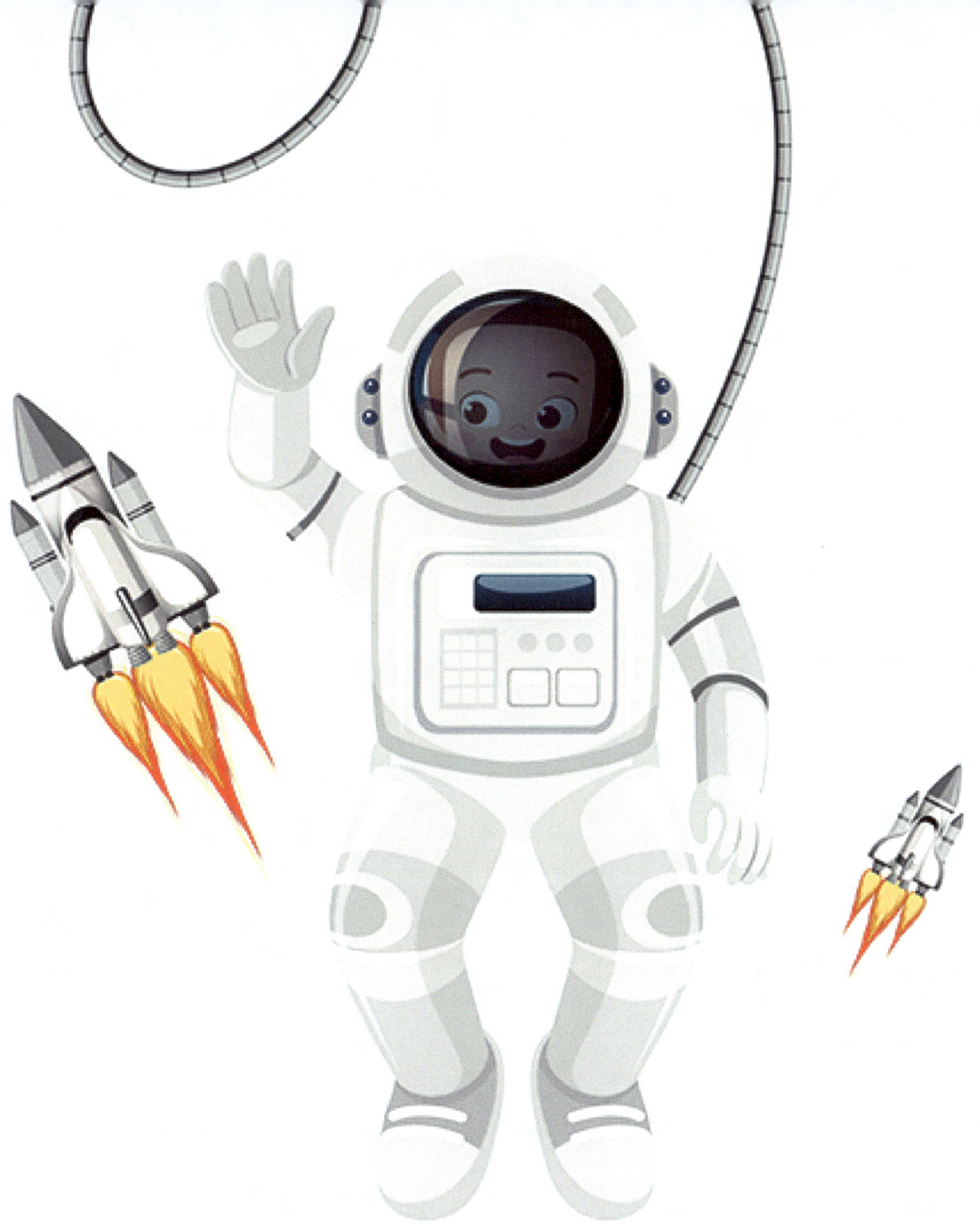

This is an ______________________

1) Astronaut   2) Engineer

This is a __________________

1) Teacher   2) Pilot

This is a ____________________

1) Scientist   2) Singer